Fast Athletes

by Cathy French

This man is fast.

He is a runner.

He is fast on the track.

3

This girl is fast.

She is a racer.

She is fast on the track.

This man is fast.

He is a bobsledder.

He is fast

on the track, too.

This woman is fast.

She is a swimmer.

She is fast in the water.

This woman is fast.

She is a rower.

She is fast

in the water, too.

This man is fast.

He is a skier.

He is fast on the snow.

This woman is fast.

She is a skater.

She is fast on the ice.

Is he fast, too?